Abraham Smith

ACTION BOOKS
Notre Dame, IN
2007

WHIM
MAN
MAMMON

ACTION BOOKS gratefully acknowledges the generosity of
the University of Notre Dame in supporting our mission
as a press.

EDITORS: Joyelle McSweeney & Johannes Göransson
ART DIRECTION: Jesper Göransson & Eli Queen
ASSISTANT EDITOR: Kristina Sigler
WEB DESIGN AND EDITORIAL: John Dermot Wood
EDITORIAL ASSISTANT: Christine Nguyen

ACTION BOOKS
Department of English
University of Notre Dame
356 O'Shaughnessy Hall
Notre Dame, IN 46556-5639
WWW.ACTIONBOOKS.ORG

whim man mammon

ISBN   0-9765692-8-2
ISBN13 978-0-9765692-8-2

Library of Congress Control Number: 2007935968

FIRST EDITION

FOR WILLIAM H. DETRA
1910-2005

FIRST LINES

WHIM
MAN
MAMMON

EVERY LITTLE METH
runt crouched in
the dark part of the culvert
every sugar road
half a bag shy
of the flour roads
every here we go crow
spoiled at the touch
of gun holes in signs
love is inside
light wet seeds
nailed into
the crawlspace
between eyetooth
and barred goon

NOTHING'S
shorn so
tight I

can't
mon-
ster it

my
kettle pocked
clay

my
loose goose
malaise

holy skillet
over yonder
love

from spain
and faint
men tone

her hair
does not stop
natural crop

clip
clip clop
good knight

MIGHT SHOULD CULL ME

cowl cow call me

artificial

heart

chucked

ambidextrous

punk

up his tree he's light

kay

see this?

when I say

cullman bama

fall

clutch

alley

dust

I am saying

age of 2 and

your pockets

nurse still

THE LADY I MOWED FOR

planted catnip
her barn half ass cathedral
to cross-eyed
pinned down ear
cats
crazies
whole barn inbred mad
white all
like a bunch of tears of sheets
over broken car parts
and lye
sun like a jellyfish
as odd as that sounds
in a landlocked mouth
I guess I am saying
a bass with a preserve
shellac up its mouthpiece
they came
weird and low
some from other barns
crooked bunched lines
like some things
anybody'd be looking to give away
they came
to the catnip patch
they rolled there they roiled
fair fair they mewled
like greased machines
like washing socks
between the broccoli
and the radishes
they came
very unlike themselves
the secret to beauty
wag egg don't aim

OR SHOULD I SAY

power dove
like a mourning lime
caught in a rub of
cheese cloth and clay

little jug head
I want to take you in

capacious dove god of any and all
just like a fresh shaved sharecropper cat green girl

lice so talk around her

pasteurized paper nail

pauper acupuncture

sweet smarting dove

like rice there is no cause to err

fly rice and

fly rice there is a combing hour there is no talking to her

SEA-WALL, A WHIRL, A WHALE PACKING HEAT, BLUE WHALE
swallowed by maelstrom, plays the rib accordion for
the pure nymphs with pistols for buttons plays and their stomps
rub jelly in the nymph's eyes Dines on road gravel falling
like confetti through saltwater, salt fractal, confetti with assembling
instructions, Catches celebratory confetti by lifting the
bottoms of one's smock, by making a baby bag, a glistening
vessel built of a shirt bowed up with happy lips of confetti,
one returns to the whale of simple times, one returns to hatch a grenade
of confetti, one plus one is one, O pinball, lightsome, marble,
the blood in the listener is built upon, is bit by the silt snake,
is all fever illimitable as the luculent fast cars are, lay hands and
   speak
silt rake tongues in the language of the child's echoing shell,
I found an arrowhead in the shale, I found an angel doll of
shale with nacre shell for eyes, lay hands on, fashion your
puppet strings from lasso meat, final ether, introducing
silent movie cellophane to the blood of life, introducing slow-mo
flower egress and cadillac pollens, I hear a cattle bell, I go hello hell
   no
into the world swim, I am a winged swimmer, I am far under purple
water, all victual, I am a catered pea, a caro astronaut,
I am favoring gills, I am launched jelly, little light gone vast,
do you read me?, primordial yawps
tuned smooth, here my cheetah jacket, here my
bones strapped to dirt clod rockets, Ali's gloves, Gandhi's underwear

CAROL, REMEMBER WHEN,

hoeing onions,
past twilight, in that half dark
half hour when
the pupils fall entirely open
and the cricket's bravado
comes on like a light in
a bathroom on a train, hoeing, the song skipped,
so, matter-of-factly, like to anything leaky or
slipped, you knelt to the situation, your heart
down there too, mango for caro, dove in for mule,

hoes a quarter inch in soil,
onions that fell light like whiskers
from snoring elders in jumpsuits
in sideburns in recliners in our common
vinyl seating Houston root,
not a sneering bone, none to press a tongue to,
a slow dervish, a sprinkle of bells
from over the hill at the Baptist
church, got it wrong, we were
the seed, the hopeful, the worthy,
soft in our bloods as old shirts,
in friendly love
with gentle lifts of crusted soils and then
let them fall like one more yes ma'am
sweet tea top off,

too much npr, we groped to find the song
that could change everything, sharpen our point,
end war, at least kill a guy with a feather
and a noun, kill him into a better guy, with
a dinged up battery powered cd player we'd dragged
into the field, I'd like to say
fought the dark, working
in a kind of fencing, a kind and
supple some fierce drill, but really we didn't do much at all,
sometimes leaning full,
worn wood handles
under our chins, sometimes laughing, balanced like this,

between yogi stork and ballroom spittoon,
born to work up a good ship of lather over worn ennui,
semi-trucks hauling ninth month leaves,
blueberry trees with a blue jay rubber dinosaur king, muscadines,
cut your mouth, fire ants, cuss them out, turnip tops
tossed in the pond, float a little like lizard wigs,
the turtles talking ancients
till they finished and waned
full on corky radishes and blighty greens,
mocker on a wire over, can't get enough Baptist bells,
does them again in miniature, beautiful little backtalk sacrilege,
may we live live live
forever far from walmart, among
the husk and husky peas and husky voiced singers
who ring among rusts and thrive on good boot gals
like tomatoes put it into drive in july, good sap blanched bones
for the hellhounds in us to snooze on
and sell the trinket dealers
treading water in the green black river,

I am stripping a downshift down in a black and white of
a sick old Woody Guthrie, his kids, his wife
ripe and round, full of life and butter
and good nature, him among them about as
opposite as board to woods, his
muscles and his memories gone to hunt seed,
bound and jerky,
his banging sound gone to brittle puff,
there with stiff and
petrified, his body a whale bone paddle thrust down in swirling cold,
   only
live thing, his cig perched like
chalk, ready to add the bird
to her song,

two weeks, two weeks, you'll call her quits, call it in, toll on
   gentler,
let the nutgrass, the fire ants, and the deer
have it, do what they will with it, yours, yours
the mockingbird dealing a deck of ring tones, yours

the hawk's one long bloodletting tool,
yours the twilit hummingbird
dexterous as a vet's right dipped in
cow ear flower sugar, yours
the cat called bear like a black hole like a portal
like a universe, yours the three mile drive through
clear cut to the wood paneled shack full of
neighbors with suspicions with tempers and fried okra with a pill bottle
of tabasco to give it some kick, and yours
your through-thick-and-thin dear, thin as wire, with those eyes like
  wine
the priests can't control, and yours the deer, when
the fences come down, 17 years after, yours, that
first twilight, the both of you in a stun, they, hedging across,
their stutter step meaning how, and you, the why on the hillside, among
  the
little stones the car kicks in the grass, a zima to
sweep you, let them have it, let yourself
have one, for a long time before the deer and dark are one,
for a long one count don't turn away, mine, mine
what you found when you knelt to that skipping song,
last branch of light to see you by, the white of your body to see you by
  as you lifted the cd and I unbent from the onions,

if Johnny Cash can't sing,
I'd like it be a beetle on the underside
keeps him to himself,
does down in the peas to
keep you from yourself
from the quiet of your bottle
from the vines with summer
over,
two belt loops
to the throats
on the trees

AGAIN THE LINE DOES NOT MOVE

again my heart
capitalizes silence
again the birds the sparrows
hunt the ground
hop like they hate ground
dare a beak
dub indivisibly
again the trees
farm the float
again the strange
man in several coats
lights his secret
face bomb red
broken ibis gear
no particular tribe of
sparrows rake the wind
soft teeth no teeth
marksman's piranha
pirate sings ha
slides his brother's sword
into the sheaths
grey sea
dinosaur blood
universe wise she's a dust mite of plexus
river into sea
rill on ice
head of a wolf
tongue of same
who's to say doesn't doodle in
the sand when licks
the crust of snow over ice
meteor designs
the cop rides the sheep
both guns out
always law
always the hopes
that they don't mean to follow

THESE LITTLE BONES

      in feet
      burn white while starlings dilate
          and ball

and sit a tree
and stick a tree
and lock a tree

trees being deathless water
emptied bones of birds
      remember water
      flirt with water
      gather in not really stone

my feet grow
nostalgic
for wings

remember when
my feet
confused
your window
    with wind

you kept the cat in the bathroom

nursed me well   it was eager worm
    gymnast's tights

    warm hands

hibiscus and jimmie rodgers

LET'S AFTER DARK AND RAIN TEA   WHEN THE NIGHT SKY HAS NO INKLING
to the apple and
        climb by the light of my hands

        when the moon begins to advertise

bird nest in the apple nest near the end I don't know who
        stays past staying no matter the wind say not even one hundred miles

this is a bullhead weather hasn't rushed it
not a word for no hand can if bird
then sky then
        trees then night then ice then dewars

                rivers washers

        moon soaps whom you choose

plenty dark
in the houses of prentice wisconsin
to keep us both polished struck slim slippery and shamed

time to go in
try to be bird come down fat sing o you all blinding

                river is a fame

flamenco in a pining for
pawn shop harmonicas

        spanish your vein

blowing wings

for the ushers of morn

        to blue up   to king

THE WAVE DICKS THE SHELL

checker chips asleep in snow

six wild birds
melt into
the bloody oreo

and they all fly down into the
ku klux klan the ku klux klan

pineal chili powder

top of every sixth thing
is melon rind melon
after teeth both
boastful truant
loose and lone

outside out back
kid licks sulfur
from match heads
scratches at earth
he's a chicken
about his mastoid

what is it? o
drop
the ladder o
molt
snake agate
stone

new mexico
not long   long

waterfall salsa dancer's
shoes pith
pit
kin

hello this thing on?
hell no no hard-on

your kiln's rather
rad red fancy

ancient mask
french kisses
fake slime

mucus spooned
down walkie talkie
dot holes

I placed the
oven mitt on
my concern and

declaring the
Z dimension

began goat
chests again

two dawns
crystallized
in how
scorpion
breaks

two women called
dawn doing
crystal meth
in montana
boon shacks

not everyone loves
fiddle music

I am pink after
wind blue
after drinking
leading the baroque
fiddle player by the chin

to the dance
at the hilt

to the hill monster

scorpion
on her side
in the tub

one hand
knut hamsun

LISTEN HER PROFOUND HOUNDS NEAR

bitter twines of silence ravel
between their hooted fists
that hold the sky just high enough
to tune her breathing harder

confession my ma's eyes fizz

7up and vodka
stirred with a blown
shotgun shell

for fear a bear will name her
teeth acorns
eyes berries
any sense of fight the thorn

flea bitter road
begging bowl presses of
everything a bear has

melon and matchsticks
in her paw

track a human palm
is lost in
blue flame jelly

white hair jim's
solitaire cards glow
by pine gum and
hard won cheese

short finger alice's
ladle of piping gravy
potato drunk driving
the edges of the pot

bears bears

soft pedal doors
bouquets of tractor mags
and char
burn barrels
for the history of a town
with fewer teeth
than the nightly
blowing trains

lost like a bird
in cotton sheets
the early cold
has wed to
and armored

she was thinking of weeding

she was humming hymns
while she hung them on the line

EAGLES
never carnal casual
the very least
eagle discloses
the plastic lie
of water
high fish foot
straining gleaming

CLOUDY BRITTLE

buckshot mailbox
empty boy

scoops snow from
wild hare prints
into a mason jar

melts it with his
future
drinking hand

ferries
high octane
to pet rabbit pens

his fiver his jackie
unzip a slug of
faster

truck dark
bar dark
turnip moon

what grown men don't
buck the
sleeves off a t

rip a five
from the table
and turn up merle

for trucks are born
to welt stones
and mourn

like haggard men
the hush of pavement
the stillborn

calving
tavern
doors

WIND THIN GIRL

sun slap
hang
ham hock
sop watt
bacon as star
half eye cat
ghosting that
catnip
sun in
warm neck milk
sun hawk
film on
slop buck
grouse pond
and fry food pond
and beaver pond
and cream cat river
woman beat shirt
on stone
lip beat out
a wild bird count
on neck and ear
throat and ear
temple and moan
lightning some
something on a stick
stick or a string
hot jeans hot jeans
she sees a hawk
thinks hawk
and float
like a bag of kittens
thrown
by the bride

1 MOUTH BREATHING

2 epithet

2 anything vinegar

2 deer end

3 jaundice cucumber

3 thorn porn

3 billeted rain

4 redbreast piss

4 willow derelict

4 throw a spark plug

4 make a wish

4 jay bust an egg

5 jay suck a rock

5 shotgun candor

4 chainsaw hymnal

6 and this train's

mighty throw

7 dust psalm

8 pie scent

9 chapped dog

10 the dog ear gravel

11 the dear god glacial till

12 bar match licked by arthritic collie

13 no no to parsimonious glee

14 string of mucus

like a rosary

took from a boy

jumping

ripped up birches

15 electric wire strung by

cussing drunk men

the thing stays

up an hour

christ is that right

you are telling me it got

unstrung bad

by them damned

green mouth ewes

sweet as the devil

milk mouth lambs
16 beers starring bees
and a vet
with a heart
like a con
15 milk glass
16 homemade battle axe
17 I'd a shot them all
17 ox and all
17 the bandage's last request
18 how one was his own house
19 how one jumped that
20 where a picture
of a kid
nipped by the war
21 soggy tooth .
22 this pain
over here
22 bacon grease
for forty days
23 white like
bare bone
24 pickled wool
25 fox gown
25 misspelled
tomato on
the grocery list
26 ref's shirt
like a perfect zebra
drinking at
the dry out
on the tv
26 ends up
crossing out
more wine
26 out from can get
27 on account of because
A.A. watching him
27 video tape

of a zebra
fleeing
bigger faster stronger
29 lint trap
tight as Mary's laugh
28 all such witless
grease and cream
29 cistern tang
30 scaffold goon
30 how about
a mosquito at night
when the light switch is
like eighty miles upriver
31 last half of Stu's marriage proposal
delivered to the ripped up birch
by where they used to throw trash
while pissing his last budweiser
32 no mention of the cattails
beating at each other
nor the gal named Sue
he first met
when he bowled a 300
and she said
long blonde hair
color of light beer
she said
nice
33 fawning chicken
32 cluck
cluck grub stab or
33 is it stone for storm gat
33 busking bucket
33 gullet pistol
34 mister yellow spotty moon
34 blood plume
34 stigmata grand
35 mouse fangs mouse ears mouse hair
36 muffled bang
37 entire attenuated crania

38 entire tibia
39 thin kid one hand
on the rabbit ears
so the fuzzy freckle
one channel tv always
deep woods temperamental
goes sudden open
clear
40 shit eating grin
kid shoveling
ice cream
into his crow
killer's mouth
40 that's a lie
bb's don't kill crows
looking away
kills crows
40 third place
speech contest
trophy precariously
against the rabbit ears
40 hell yes the
A-team
40 spread a lot of lead
but nobody gets hurt
40 grandpa said
41 never mind the metatarsal
42 never mind the metacarpal
43 mindfield shouts of rodentia
clenched in the death paw
43 hawk
43 hawk
44 first squeaks of fire
45 o cairn in bone
46 cold rains from crows
47 pickled dust
47 A.A. info bled
by rain
47 enormous makeshift creeks

of marrow
48 the mirror
no one has ever
written in lipstick on
like in
the movies
49 dust upon upon
51 rag sings
sad to see him go
52 son's hair
packed into tube socks
tied to lath
tethered to cool golden
garden
soil
52 seen on tv
is a good way
to keep
deer off crops
52 be back
how did he say
sometime
like in the movies
53 human hair
rammed in socks
53 dreams a long shapely
dream of a man
cussing out two deer
55 licorice
55 greyhound exhaust
56 leaving indianapolis
at 6:43
54 while real bucks
and fawns burn
through dream soft
turnips carrots peas
55 darkest night
56 never mind
57 sleeping

58 divorcees
59 coyote's bright leg
under moon's no legs
one good cheek
60 60 60 60 60 60
st. louis
first time
in for
chips and a coke
61 first pretty
woman
spotted
62 thought she
winked
62 a barred grin
63 thought she might
if I asked right
play glade my lanolin

I'LL GALLEY HOLD SPIDER LEGS
I'll garland them with peppercorns

if they're grim
glands swollen
eyes like something
half bled
coming up the long
winding
scary movie
winter drive

I'll gladly galley hold
I'll hot peppercorn

beam them
providentially

honey hang

rise   to glide to rise

I HAD MY SHREW ON

why lady let me
shy my hands away

let my blood run white
as nacre
let it quiver
in the east side hole

the day
I found you
in my place
stapled to the dark
astride the sofa
melted crayon in your
left hand
the left
why do I remember that?

little details
like not the right and red
painted statues
bleeding
crayon dust
in my wren dusts

the truth was
you were
a sawed in half shark
in salt
on snow

a loom of ice and lice and ice and snow

SEA GULLS CLOSE THEIR
time for dummies bodies
over our numb roof and snow closes its
prince's nil over the toenail yes of sand

the cartoon where
the painted bird head
opens her celery

I mean that meek mouth opens when   surprise   celerity

celebrity kandinsky   closet

salamander jackhammer juniper   bones

YES THE

bless the
train eyeballs designed from
glass might be on them and the socket
is rude if exposed so hurry them man
if you will to
japan by way the second fat fish hollow roll
I think they're romantic
tricky baby
factoring the h off the then
ten robins
they don't do much when it's chill
huddle up and fluff
no gladly your foot my foot
never been to the city
so forcefeed me
your man in florida
flyfishing
where I wonder
in some aquarium?
real live country singer's boots
on the hook
a little burnt
little bitter
but I didn't mean
acid butter
the trains
mean peace is in mosey
blowing plastic bags
one branch higher
my one true love
in turn a brightened
posture amen

NO ONE SPEAKS OF THE STRIDENT CALLS

of sparrows robins et cetera
because the song
and the body
almost
don't connect
beautiful little hairy
shotgun shell versus
something pinched and overbearing
now the dove
no one calls it
adam's apple
on a war vet
aslumber in his recliner
adam's apple of cellophane

I guess
one can get behind doves better
their homespun circle of flannel
fingered over red black corkboard

owl in a bottle
the color of lead

king me   this one's modest jest

HER AND I HAD BEEN IN THE VINEGAR

okay   I tossed the phone

I am blaming 1981
through 1989

that night I came home
after watching her

soften another man's
smoke stack bricks

none of it even half way
depraved   raving

I needed a smacking kiss   needed a not shot skunk
to talk to about how to walk bent and slug

needed a coat made of stickers
from store bought fruits

I did not know   point of fact   what knead dew
I saw my chair   my good old

antique not unkind chair
had long been kindling

since the preacher
had given his spare rocker

it was a straight back antique chair
it was not good for

balling up in   call it crying lonesome
lightning monsoon eaves

okay I picked up my chair and
tuned into the sweet gum trees

best way to say it is   have you seen
it's a wonderful life when

jimmy stewart's george bailey
realizes he's totally fucked
did you know it was actually
over 90 degrees when they

filmed that flick had a hard time
keeping even fake snow I had that look

hard time with also a beetle a demented kid
had poured kerosene on for my eyes

I took of the chair and threw it against
the sweet gum trees I followed through

chuffing angry ground ivy poison ivy
all earth a chill flame old time scottish for

donning stiff old cold pants in the morning is chilblains
lord knows I had them ill no amen

raw itch filth monstrous I
launched the chair deeper

fell in a ravine little death legs
tickled my tomorrows

there was tart clay there were the atomic
lice of animal eyes I dragged

the chair at my hip kept slinging it
I carried it like it was wanted for

the million heisted the day
the last good deal went down

I heaved the chair
towards every tree from here to

part ways through georgia that's the way
it felt in my mind the chair didn't know

what to do the chair was fine because it was
old therefore a solid chair it didn't have experience

it's sort of like flipping your wig
on someone who's had a wonderful life they don't know

what you are they look at you like okay
a falling meteor made of an orphan a thin mint I mean

that's the landless scythe because I was
working at the farm decent strong hands okay

I shotput the chair I lobbed it and it held
straddling a sweet gum it clung to the branches clung to the bark

part like it was making love to the tree and part like it was
an anorexic bear just sort of trying to get away

a lot sad I was a pity racy sight it was I couldn't reach
to work the scene better a light rain set in

I waited for a deal of time under that sweet gum tree
waiting just waiting to see if maybe

the chair wanted to come back to me I took off my cap I made a sweet talk
to my chair in the tree but the chair didn't budge

the chair was proud and pissed part like it was telling the tree psst
see that guy he's no good part like it was waiting for the tree

to sit down and part like it was just that infernal tree sticking
its leggy tongues out at me I tell you that chair

didn't come rain came boot hard old news heart char I was
my shoes my shoes stunk in the morning morse code for

creaking bucket my hank boots slipped
I kicked a coal caught a cadillac

pig pig sparrow

HOLDS HOLDS TO   THE SCARING LEAVES

the house sides   poultice to the million dents   and the bits
of glass scattered like saccharine upon the dirty streets of Tuscaloosa
what is lamentable is joined to the underside of my skin   sweet scar
  sap din Train
of bad luck and giddy fortune   Get me out train   Train howitzer
  cannibalized for
parts and made again as something to Lick and grow ride from   carnival
  of
plastic wide things northern lighting on the no light tree   I see a
  queasy stair
and ascend Train of unforgivable you don't know what train
with a tine of jello on its capsized puppy law train of hide me away
Train of tunelessness brought back upon itself until the tools all go
Mush   that little dog on the wide stair that stair kibitzing with the
compass that compass needle carrying on
with the junk   the junk dog has his stuff all up in the can of beans
  Train of
bean plants northern lighting on the no light trees   Train of up and
  train of
good enough and train of waking with the salt rim eyes   With the salt
  rim eyes
By your last let wet warm exhalation by your cotton sack almost wavy
  lipids I find
an infinite tongue hammock I hammer my soft slow in my elbow for pillow
even if all night the train insinuating itself in discarded chicken
bones   just melon juice just ka pa pa in the dream That thing I lick
as I
save cows from flood in that dream popsicle running down my arm
that blue dot on my thigh   fast and Fast

THE ACTUAL PILL BOTTLE OF THE SEA, ACTUAL PILL BOTTLE

oversexed by the motions of the fog, keeping the fishermen in,
their café playing cards slipping like wild animals
from woods to grass, we speak
in rote pride of what's worth
reviling in the
domesticate; transport selected for
over taste; cards slicked
from hand to
hand, something of the grease
of the café eggs is
hushing the cards as the players
husk least ink from the king's nose; when they sleep they wed
small queen hair; gambling suits
the fishermen; also a mustache; a mustache as slang for
whiling away time; dolphins fit the water;
the muscle of the sea; the good leg; the medicine—the water takes the
   dolphin
for a bootlegging good time;
pretty obviously; pretty natural, whereas I struggle
onto my legs, in the morning, boil
the water so it will dream
a slow moving Oklahoma tornado viewed on tv
into my cup, rain wind dust mud, they found hay
like a rash, under his skin; they found, in the malls, a stale lunch, a
   gallon
bucket of mediocrity; I paint my teeth with suds; I purchase penny
   candy,
I pedal, they are really not chasing me; it is me and the birdsong;
there is something, nothing to it; we are owed what we give; we are not
made for a tree anymore; we are
not made to see god in fire; we are not made with smoke in our hair; but
   we
are not made to use our eyes upon the vast crunch of the city; we seem
a little made for holding; we just need to be left alone to feel alone
and
remember our arms

MY DEAR SWEET INSANE RABBIT

I would say rabbi but the t is in texas
and texas is incommunicable
hate dallas or ought to
if you haven't been there let a sick guy
breathe in a bag
and then stick your head in the bag
let there be much rolling of eyes
I guess to roll an eye is to risk
blindness for he who don't
keep a camera on the bum
da dum dum dum
I am just gonna go over here and go over heads a time
cool killness a time
felt it some but mostly in my snake tail boots
beat the sidewalk street clear
in front of those low fort worth houses
women rinsed their brushes
again the octopus or the giant squid
brown hairs rinsed down
I am thinking of a basin placed upon a whale
gents with burnt heels
stepping there
such vast slickness jelly leg medicine
take the word back out of the mustache
I am thinking of a politician
named bert
curt bert
with a mechanical pencil
for a penis
and a buoy
unsalted as yet
for heart
dear rabbit
do you remember when
you played with knives played with crumbs
how many hours
milled past grist
trying to force

a certain roll when really
if the white bears
and us two dirty as a beard
upon a whaling captain
come into a city
in 1890
to see about a property
west some miles
his teeth iridescent green
his hands or in the colloquial his mitts
white as blubber but he does nothing
in the big smoke worth mentioning so I will tell you
he coughed twice because he was nervous and he bought the land and he
shot a buck on the land
three years after
no go down
on history
for he was just
another manatee with
two porcelain dolphins
for lungs
that's well over forty lines and I have not done a thing
about the eaves shocked with snow melt on march third
the zoo man's stethoscope
on a giraffe's legs
the snow through like new eaves
a wash of gorgeous gaffs
a sass on god a talking sash
we won't have
to sound a ballast
come a first light pin
amended the beach   did we not   at one a.m.?
where was I   a little paperclip ship
and were you not a little paper burp
shore I could not see
hugged
until our buttons pearled
thank god
our buttons were not living

perhaps kelp when I said that   hurt you   we did not kiss you did not
   want to throw your necklace
on a wolf with no good idea for his neck
light to end in knots
don knotts   sweet funny man   his adam's apple   generous applause
we watched the sea
the lights across did the water in winks
we watched and we held
I felt your heart against
my right nipple
it went one deer
foot down
in the peas
one panther paw
a dross
in leaves

THEIR BODIES ARE FIXED
they can't run lines
hitch is in the bone
they do the ferret rock
they do the shepherd horse eating
piecrusts off waves amen

for the tree is the squirrel is the amnesia

what I am
the flabby
terse skid of the almost tree if you will only
forget as animals not well versed no big ass
statue in the humors
fuck it forget what
where ends in tree if the deer does not cudgel the wit
sap out of the darling limp reed good to rip if boy and wicked reed

THICKETS OF SLEEVES

sparrow I am no
intense fan of

o you rang a bell
searching
the penny dish
for a dime
is old hat and down

I am just going to
meek cat one
little mewling bomb

I am no ox
not parapet
no fancy

no moon cow
treating
moos to
manacles

another dead level
ground swell
of shivering

I shall stitch
a hat
in the shape
of how you feel

heart of the bush
blink and the
sparrow blurs

I shall shell-weave you
a serf from
my spain sun
faded sleeves

the sunset
butters
the criminal
maybe gauche baby
but your eyes
sparrow cat me

who will know you
in that hat
this scarf

surely not that man
bent over
his belts

his sheep are clouds
lawyers shot and
sucked the freshets from

my mower revved
I joust the outhouse
for your love

your 1 x 1
on my shut eyes

are you the one
cot soaked with gasoline?

actual feathers
actual sparrows

scary crows

prayerful guns

that lizard thing anew

VENISON TOUGH AS
my late great grandfather's vodka shoes

blues for us plate lickers
told to chew

with a chick-sized
spiral of white bread

taught to spool buck tenderloin
by tender I mean easy as

blocks of unthawed sod
told to spiral the wedges

inside something softer
so it felt like done

when really the meat
would not go

old christ in deer old
gramps in deer

lay me down gentle
in the half moon

in the kitchen wall
where grandpa bill's

fist sprang the last
day they tanked vodka

orphan tough plug of
what was meant to

leap a spark fence and
sugar foot in our corn

doubtful flesh
I let stay awhile then

coughed and rocked in
the blue tulip napkin
for the different eye dog
whose blue one was wet with

a future in mouthing
and gnashing

dog mouth sang back
all wing

my dad put a bend
in the din

shocked licks of his plate
smacked it swabbed it

lips like a horse
on late april ground

just so cool woods knew
who we were

crows and the slugs
thunder and tinder

in the big oak never
a nickel in creases

it wouldn't have mattered
if the president had

opened his checkbook
if christ had strung a lit ladder down

just so one bone in one ear
dipped to our tender

labor all together a river
of licking noises

by freaking god
all of us until they glistened

ice floes under sun
down rivers named for

wolves and wolfish men
whose tin dip cans

whispered full moons
in work jeans

patched four ways with pants
I ripped the ass on

kneeling to my first
still warm deer

my knife just so
my hand slid in

and all the plates
began a claim

on hopeful
blues

vultures and crows
sky-locked

waiting
to fall to steaming

chains I'd spilled
by skittish aspen

by blood became
man hauling love

to clear pasture to
cow bone road to

our doe skull yard
hard with dogs

risen on hind legs
lapping the wind

WE BOTH SPLIT

like summer melon
hit by a part
from a washing machine

yes seeds but no
seeds to bean
the oils from

I run olive
oil all in my glasses

make it so I only see in sleep

wedge of bread
masks the crow
a clown you know
fat white nose

pecked once
and dropped
from yonder pine

your smashing legs
uncrossed

god your dropping foot
evens the ground

HERON
hearing me
say o

my

gathers stiff
slims its grey

if we could see light
teenaged
but bounce back
that's it

gathers in one
sweet swift click

like a lance
shoved up the ghost

like a lance
falling from
the armpit of
the ballerina

I straighten
and suck in
and sing at mud

my bad bird

you're no lance

and I am no
olive pit
rub

HONEY HAWK KNOCKS GIN DRINKS AGAINST ME
for rights
to the sweet talker's scent
me and this hawk knock around
time runs when I think of
basketball I think of sweat
bong times run
out

hawk does not
win I win take that sucker
knocks my tailbone my belt buckle
my thigh flesh my dream of hawaii
all knocked by hawk
into an ATM
corner of 5th and spring
I tell you my body
by the fact of my jarred body
keys the ATM unlocks it and cash soft cash
in multiples of twenty
we're talking radio wave soft
sprays like wings
like a chicken getting taken by a hawk

sad top hat men
I don't know not afraid to
pop their pants their backs
reaching down

there is this bridge gun grey
all of us lads
down on the river
scrubbing fine
hairless gleaming bodies
with twenties
and I don't hardly

have to tell you
what's next cuz

a mouse like a shoe of rubies
or I got extra feisty and bit
a mouthful of your dress
and sang it to the floor

a mouse a mile away
shakes her spinal cord in hot
restitution wings
baked bread wings

break of aspen
dreamboat honolulu
seahorse with a smile

nun throat
late light
amen
her ninth skin
as mica in trees

I smoke
twenties rolled in aspen leaves
exhale a nervous house
okay the hawk for the door

don't knock
that's death

just swivel in
around the wing

OUR OWL FACE SUN

on earth my stone

stinks with sun

this sun palm sea

hey worthy mud

hushed throe

without egress

sans any actual

thought I throw my name

in stone to sea

the sea does not bleed

sand forgives

forgets

hey   hey

HER COAL NOSE

winter coat button eyes
snap out of pines
like a lady
at a gala ball
roar of freight of cow
going down to
roaring freight of
dolphins all
worms deader
than the nails
they gave rise to
all books
nervous in
cheek spark breeze
mother leaps leaps
long thorn bushes
zapping wires
pillowy ferns
her perfect white
skid ground
grain crown
double monkey
pair of bones
roll back into the
shaky stow
of pines
open wide
good now
bite down
good god
nip that donkey
crossdressed
as sunset you
slap it on you
pull the plough

SPIKE FACE CROW

come out of no

and right hand

sky go down

den den time

time swallow horse

time swallow hollowness

crow carry shell

water to pine

is ten then sixteen wing for torn

slicked out

flanks of river

cut sheet

bit the shell until the snow

o deer

used to call it

dulcet impairment

dusk clasps

is new some

easy easy

carotid

exhalation

at least a lit

hang

little as a lantern's child

spark it

on boy

by path by river

in his is he

first

fingers cloud

first in bone form

is ten fingering three

skips stone

he alone is

when stone hits

what water

comes to him is

blue hair

electrician's wire

new king

blue skin

dove dead to legs

he walks the river

river's wet leg

down in

down to where

the dead are

copper

firings

THEY DON'T LOOK TO GO

midst the flock
when the whole
silk sock crowd
tilts elsewhere

none eye the other and
end-stitch the jelly there

pre-turn they feel
ideal curtains
peep in blood

in faith

a lacey tectonics
a whispery lip
a wheel in blood
in the eyeball of
eyeballs kiss
wheels of jewels
jewels sails
taste shapely
on paper
there's no way
to bale
these jewels

torn from same
torrent sane
so in skein

fly by way of mending

the man the tree the day   man tree day   mantra day oooo!

adios clouds
of rum

deus ex machina

WAITING FOR THE BIRDS AGAIN

a cool wind
I wait and one
alights along my
double knots

clasps a seed
moon white
in his maw

cocks his head

tiny black eyes shining

hello little man

the seed doubles the beak

kisses ether
fiddly dee
and grace

to oak
to melt
the birth key of
the high and mighty sunflower

yellow
on his breath

his sweet gear
his cageless brain

wing flick like
somebody gambling

9 card shines river water and lye

to rub
the loser
from the floor

1

THE SNAKE HANDLER PRIMPS HIS HANDLEBAR MUSTACHE
in the mirror beside the poster of fit girls in short shorts
in the mountainous west the girls are mountainous

narrow canyon tin canoe

piss beer ring on her left hand now that's just bear piss
ring or lack thereof lets him know
should he bust out the vanilla million goad

I can dance just choose to dine on wall

interesting shadow tell me how was it you came to the nicks on
your vandals your bevy of green prints the catkins your boils

fat hauls from craps games beyond the wall there is this pitiful over
and over again busted out window and wind shine off wheat

silvered by plexiglas severed from his handlebar he pounds his round
  fat
hard on the wood bar ouch out

crows

bad checks bad breath judges

flat tires

question is

how far can he go on the rims

answer cling cling cling cling

                a while

2

the arsonist and barista are trading explanations of steam

he says inverted cone
she says ghost octopus

watch this   lowers his voice
into her empty earring hole
leveling with her
lights his toothpick

oh she says meaning
his scar   his gondola long ways burn

she says   in the air   with her creamy fingers
fixing the drink   she has written   quite meekly

the gar in the sea is longer than wide and pretty
as the killer when the killer was nine

3

the painter
returned from the loo
his return form good
see his zipper's snug
sews a sprinter
in his journal

pigeons eating ballplayer's
toenail clippings
fear they hang

4

kiss the barista
click of the lock
satisfies

iron knob is
the arsonist

the siren the
arsonist
ironing god

5

snake handler
under a lime wedge moon
dirties his boots
for the painter
who's set up his easel
in spring's first dispositive drool

good the painter burrs   good god the
python belt now

6

mouse mouse   his brush at play

the handler in his head
the wheat was a dream
the dream was a woman on fire with dice

o half toboggan sway to lower back I ride
the fifty lotus   let her   my hand small

I show   remember to next time   picture of the robe   I don
sash and brine shrimp with right powder no trouble at all

7

the killer
in jail
dreams a hole
he did not
commit
and so
like a bird his
half dream
committed he
beats
the land
like a bell

I AM FAMOUS IN CHINA

for paralyzing figurines
in little pills of glass
that's sweet evening
under my fingernails
I am a glassblower I blow glass
did I ever tell you that? Announcement
I've never known freedom like this before

Have I ever blown glass
for you in China? okay Lila let me
dish this to you in a little less than my standard nasal tone
Ok you're in my dreams I am dreaming a technological horse
I am dreaming I am emailing myself running to you
Lila why aren't we eloping? shall blow you a little glass thing
little glass lamb for you baa baa Lila I won't do
snakes biting the heel of a sharecropper's gambled for stallion
just a little four peg legs lamb keeping the sun a little
like any righteous living tuft of cotton would do Lila I am
slipped free from the natural pledge of mouth
to grass to dew Ain't I whistling good now?

I shall dine on your laughter here on in
Swish your plates whilst you are out and about Is it too late
to blow glass? back at the house are ample supplies the old
Maria marsh full of harsh biting bugs is off
treating her instrument like a snakebite victim in the London subway
so we are alright that way Lila summers
the house resounds with the red sounds of she and her streetmade friends
they're in the next room doing battle with the succulent chops of the
  sea

I like younger women Lila Open! did you ever have the great idea of
hooking up with a bearded galoot in fat winter boots with one thing
on his mind and that ain't glass? a 60 something and a 20 something
put us together and we are almost dead Let's us quick then the Maria
  monster is out
huffing gas with the fire eaters in the east side of Peru

Honey when I see you I feel open like o I am a pen and swine I am
   swine in a
cobbled pen we are talking bits of old signboard and bits of old bones
nailed together with some house fire nails into an oval and me o pig pink
sigh sigh sigh sigh
I await your discarded toast edges it's best to go truffling in autumn
   Lila
scorches my glass blowing equipment Absolutely eats it up with flame

I am as they say in the jelly commercials a Jealous man a jellyous man
it's toasty delicious here in my Walt Whitman beard Lila electric
this house rocks in summer and I bet you can guess what the Mar is up on
   to in here
I'd like to burn her one time
by the fact of you and I hand in handing our way
down the Break Water shall secure our picture
walking into jelly sunset reds I do truly scorch and blast and rave
I hell palm the art materials when I get jealous pissed if I can hear
Maria and her boys screwing in the next room then chicken dogs spoon my
heart I am not saying
anything about spooning dogging nailing screwing just our
two frames nailed into the jelly sunset as we ease our
trivial selves down the Break Water at sunset and I shall
by the miracle of computers transpose that picture onto a calendar and
every month every moment damn the moths my dear
toast honey eye honey
every day will be
Us Sunset Break Water hand in Hand

I like baubles little critters stupefied by glass Did I ever say my
   beard is
taiga come you and prance
Let me impersonate vast warm towels
pressed further and further into your personal space Let me impersonate
four foot across moths mide of hot wet towel pressed further and further
towards your very original visage the trivia is almost up my hand
   tires
of flipping you off it's time to lose glass blower's fingers in your
shiny rock album hair Lila when the moon gets busy in your hair

I want to ask my hand to be a semi truck because between you and me
your mane is totally highway and I can't help but roll windows down
joint smoke coupling with stars   you stain the night
Lila the sound of a semi with one smoking wheel

I am in an open relationship   together we are almost dead
I want to drive   I know a little place   I want to pull off at the rest
  stop called your ear
leave a little pipe on the top of your ear   Balance it there   Lila in
  summer
in Iowa City and now you have gone too far   when you housesit
when you see outside your house sitting establishment
the weltering night sky   endless sky   digital strokes of fireflies
Let it be that you wend a little think to your dear old Wade
your Wade down on the pier   smashed on the smoke   I don't care you might
very well huff your very own weed smoke in Iowa   yes paint me
in your sweet zonked head   firefly pigment for paint   oink oink   yes
stable me in your inaccurate haze   neigh neigh   your limbs embalmed by
satisfying palpitating fireflies   but Lila   lady how
wildebeest can you be Ms. Russia?   unwrap those marble arms
from your Lover boy man and
Wink a little kiss   he shall not miss it   Truth!   it will win itself
  here   as sure as
the light of day is the nark of all scars
One winged Montanan
kiss for your dear old Baked man standing
slightly portlier Quixote
upon the pier   before this vast ditch of sea
whose old wax
cylinder I've scratched into becoming you   your hair   you   your hair
  you   your hair
you   your

I REMEMBER
every bird that sings
I am brief and lame

crooked grapes incense
the cardinal's crooked cheaps

the spit white hands of
old folks doling sads
to cardinals jays

it's okay
because it's cheap

I know
we young keep seed in sex
and wander
unaware of war

vast lank skin flicks

THOUGH I'VE BEEN FAITHFUL

my heart cheats
when it beats
like a sandwiched
grenade

it was I
who thought
the squirrels are
high temperatures
given to
grandfather clocks till
they burst

I who drawled
the squirrels are jangled bits
of grandfather clocks
bitching
over
dimes

O PENGUINS HOW LOVELY

a dove in a tux for sure
and did they carry trays with salmon sandwiches
and thimbles of twinings and cucumber bits
like good little waiters
aren't they smart like fluent in six languages
or am I thinking of blue whales yes I know it
greats are both lovely and moltenly
irritating when they eat for example chicken
my great uncle opens to entire wings
older lower flying times
asks after the washski after the barnski asks after
eye-talian dressin asks who it was what last saw
that neighbor of ours
the big dumb fat swede and
the hay ride cost a nickel do you think
we had a nickel? no we shore didn't
though he can lord one tough over us
none have known
flour sack underwear
to nettle the privates
as we saunter through barcelona
lonesome and detached from the war
ploosh ploosh went his niece's arms into washing suds
in other folks' houses that's how they made ends meet after
max got run over by a hay wagon and lived
yes it's a shark vertebra I was dreaming it was
me slow dancing with a macaroon breath manatee
was the manatee put that ice shaving in my ear
shark   swish of our boots
shark   peck on the cheek   swish of our boots
shark and lying on my kitchen table   yes I see the seismic denture shine
sure true italians at times wear twinkling pink getups
and you and your diesel gasoline jacket sensibilities
likely take that as unmanly so to caution
before these reign in softest dove cough mornings
I am ragamuffin hip hip italian from the next day down
don't want you wincing like lemon took to loving up your eyes
when I spill out of the car into your carriage house

in a day glow green cowboy shirt constellated with rhinestones
like greg brown says people say small things
when they stay too long in little rooms
o I am at least a gooseful of hours outdoors everyday
the sun these days is geeked in bees dandified curative elixir
say now what is it the curate uses on his bleeding gums?
answer bee's knees
bowling ball talc and the penguin joke
concerning the penguin and hyena
down at the rodeo it goes without saying
my grandpa's head is one helluva circus
never was a religious man
people say he walked with deer
tickled their chins
flipped kernels of field corn
off his thumb
in and down their dog nun hatches
alzheimer's now sad because
never would have wished to live this far from deer
happy when he doesn't pine
happy when his bed is
cut from skin of moon
how much you need?
and bart and brett and starr and favre
a five a hundred
million million
my ball playing shoulder pads sleeping
thousand dollar bills
I sign a dream in ball playing turf
and pretty gals with dentist drills
dig up my scores
patch them in their watered patch and never
run short again
listen to my grandpa
thin as howled down birches
sawing off another
stretch pants aphorism
other day he says and he
paints his eyes up and down to where he is silken and invisible

could walk through walls into the blue pens if he wanted to
into the 69 ounce shit bag of cola if he wanted to
lifted to the painted mouth of the lady in the office who's just now
licking an envelope full of tenants' checks
costs 3000 a month to stay in this assisted hoohaa
would have wanted us to
put a little t-shirt on him and send him out in
zero wind chill saying go go on gramps
go on out and find the pin sheared off the tractor last june
paints his eyes up and down
last night jesus come by
you know jesus is back and he's all around
I see him sort of sashay in and sing
jesus bill they're making electric cars on the cold side of the moon
no joke and a raving coffee gnashing
flashlight coffee kind of guy jesus has his
leg up on my bed and he's keeping time on
my sternum and he's frailing on this little
guitar you would have thought was half dead
he says this guitar was once an orphan what got the mange
he says
you got good belly muscles seems you laughed
a lot in your prime mind and I says
cut it with the eye-talian dressing drizzled on
iceberg lettuce speeches bub
and I says the most pained thing ever happened was
brother clyde in that mummy ice down by the river
and no I never hardly laughed I was yelling
goddamn it this fucking christmas tree
my ma died giving birth to me why I
swing a heavy axe in the month of february
see then jesus sorta put his slipper up off my belly
and onto the side of the bed to where I could
contrive my arm under the bed and
jesus says I will just do a little elvis number for you and I says
fine that'll be fine I might just call in some of my
good old great big dumb swede friends if you don't mind
o bless his fig herring heart
jesus closes his eyes to say he don't mind plus to

try and   you know   calling collect connect
and that's when I snake skin my arm under the bed
and come out with this great big lug of an old tire iron
and rare it up
and just when he lays into how I ain't nothing but an old hound dog
wham   see I clock jesus right over his fool head
and awoosh see   he separates into a million and a million
breaks down fast to moths butterflies
sparks sparring gloves stars footballs
which I catch one of the footballs
and make a dash for the end zone
where this band is playing
I can't say for fact the toot
but I do say galoots smooching tubas
and clyde swinging a fountain drink
drumstick down on frozen birds
and how I sorta slipped off
into the silver innards
of that music playing machine

WHIM MAN MAMMON

```
secret soil coital
the dove there
sounds blonde as
whipped oil
please appeal to
wimpling skies
journeying trees
there is but one fence
bone true and
one blockhead dog
inside
to rend
the smarts
of trees
at journey's end
```

ACKNOWLEDGEMENTS

The author would like to thank the editors of the following journals, where several of the poems, sometimes in slightly different arrangements, first appeared: *The American Poetry Review, Cream City Review, Fence, jubilat, Ninth Letter, Northwest Review,* and *Shankpainter.*

THANKS TO:
Linda Kavanagh, Richard Smith, Monica Detra, Meggan and Eddy Meisegeier, Erin Kavanagh, Jessica McBride, Pam Carazo, Dianne Smith, David Floyd, Joel Brouwer, Steve Timm, Carol Eichelberger, Nathan Parker, Ashley and Scott McWaters, Grace Sullivan, John Pursley III, Donald Revell, C.D. Wright, Sophia Karstonis, Jillian Weise, Robin Behn, Craig Arnold, Sonya Feher, Mike Henry, Dan Towler, Abigail Green, Kristen Schiele, and Jerry Goldberg,

SPECIAL THANKS TO:
Joyelle and Johannes

ABOUT THE AUTHOR

Abraham Smith hails from Ladysmith, Wisconsin. He holds an MFA in Creative Writing from the University of Alabama. He's published and performed widely, including poems placed in *Hunger Mountain, DIAGRAM, New Orleans Review,* and *Typo,* and feature gigs at the Bowery Poetry Club, South-by-Southwest Music/Film Festival, and the National Poetry Slam. He was a 2004-2005 Writing Fellow at the Fine Arts Work Center, Provincetown, MA. He lives light on the land in Wisconsin, Brooklyn, and everywhere in between.

ACTION BOOKS CATALOG

2007 / 2008 ACTION BOOKS TITLES

WHIM MAN MAMMON
by Abraham Smith
ISBN 0-9765692-8-0
ISBN13: 978-0-9765692-8-2

THAUMATROPE
by Brent Hendricks
illustrations by
Lisa Hargon Smith
ISBN: 0-9765692-9-9
ISBN13: 978-0-9765692-9-9

PORT TRAKL
by Jaime Luis Huenún
translated by
Daniel Borzutzky
ISBN: 0-9799755-0-6
ISBN13: 978-0-9799755-0-9

MOMMY MUST BE
A FOUNTAIN OF FEATHERS
by Kim Hyesoon
translated by Don Mee Choi
ISBN: 0-9799755-1-4
ISBN13: 978-0-9799755-1-6

2006 ACTION BOOKS TITLES

YOU ARE A LITTLE BIT HAPPIER THAN I AM
by Tao Lin
Winner of the 2005
December Prize
ISBN: 0-9765692-3-X
ISBN13: 978-0-9765692-3-7

YOU GO THE WORDS
by Gunnar Björling
translated by
Frederik Hertzberg
Scandinavian Series #2
ISBN: 0-9765692-5-6
ISBN13: 978-0-9765692-5-1

THE EDGE OF EUROPE
by Pentti Saarikoski
translated by Anselm Hollo
Scandinavian Series #3
ISBN: 0-9765692-6-4
ISBN13: 978-0-9765692-6-8

LOBO DE LABIO
by Laura Solórzano
translated by Jen Hofer
ISBN: 0-9765692-7-2
ISBN13: 978-0-9765692-7-5

2005 ACTION BOOKS TITLES

THE HOUNDS OF NO
by Lara Glenum
ISBN:0-97656592-1-3

MY KAFKA CENTURY
by Arielle Greenberg
ISBN:0-97656592-2-1

REMAINLAND: SELECTED POEMS OF AASE BERG
by Aase Berg
translated by
Johannes Göransson
Scandinavian Series #1
ISBN:0-97656592-0-5